GRUMMAN C·A·T·S

GRUMMAN C·A·T·S

Michael O'Leary

OSPREY
AEROSPACE

Published in 1992 by
Osprey Publishing Limited
59 Grosvenor Street, London W1X 9DA

ISBN 1 85532 247 1

Editor Tony Holmes
Page design by Paul Kime
Printed in Hong Kong

Front cover Tucked in tightly alongside the camera-ship, Howard Pardue in his XF8F-1 Bearcat flies a two-ship formation with the Confederate Air Force's FM-2 Wildcat. Hailing from Bethpage, New York, the Bearcat was designed around the combat reports written by Wildcat pilots, who had tackled the might of the Imperial Japanese Navy during 1942. Sleek, slippery and overpowered, the Bearcat is arguably the finest piston-engined fighter ever built

Back cover The largest of all the 'prop cats', the F7F Tigercat saw no actual combat during World War 2, unlike the F6F Hellcat, which was ordered from Grumman on that same June day in 1941. This pristine aircraft is owned and operated by the Lone Star Flight Museum, who are located in Galveston (where else could they be based!), Texas

Title page A mixed bag of veteran and vintage warbirds. Ag pilot Gerald Martin leads the pack with the Confederate Air Force's (CAF) FM-2 (BuNo 55585) N681S, followed by two Corsairs, two Sea Furys, a P-38 and a nearly invisible F8F Bearcat during an October 1976 photo sortie over Harlingen, Texas

For a catalogue of all books published by Osprey Aerospace
please write to:

**The Marketing Department, Octopus Illustrated Books,
1st Floor, Michelin House, 81 Fulham Road, London SW3 6RB**

F6F-5 BuNo 77722, mounted in front of the Naval Reserve section of Andrews AFB in Maryland, has been sited in that location for many years. With the value of our few remaining World War 2 vintage aircraft so high, it would be hoped that this F6F will be removed and preserved inside a building instead of being subjected to the very harsh Maryland weather

Introduction

With the decreased threat of world-wide military action from the collapse of what was known as the Soviet Union, American military contracts have been drastically cut back. One company to feel the stinging effects of these cutbacks is Grumman Aerospace which saw its superb F-14D Super Tomcat dropped and the final A-6 Intruder delivered to the Navy.

Grumman has built some of the finest naval warplanes of all times and this volume takes a look at the Grumman series of 'Cats – the Widlcat, Hellcat, Tigercat and Bearcat. For good measure a few Avengers and other Grumman warplanes have also been added.

What is depressing is the fact that so few of the many combat aircraft designed and built by Grumman exist today. The few that do survive and still fly are the products of a small group of individuals who, for various reasons, wanted to keep a famous segment of aviation history alive and flying. To this small band, all aviation enthusiasts owe a debt of thanks.

Michael O'Leary is the associate publisher of a group of aeronautical magazines. This is his eighth book for Osprey.

Right With the right Pratt & Whitney R-2800 just kicking over, F7F-3 (BuNo 80483) N6178C prepares to launch from Duxford, England, for an aerobatic display in the hands of Paul Warren-Wilson. Operated as tanker 43E, the Tigercat saw service with Cal-Nat Airways and Sis-Q Flying Service. Stored for several years at Santa Rosa, California, the Tigercat was delivered to Britain by air, arriving on 13 November 1988 to become the only example of its type in the UK and Europe

Contents

F4F Wildcat

Above Right from the start, it should be stated that all the flyable aircraft featured in this chapter are actually licence-built Eastern Aircraft FM-2 Wildcats. Unfortunately, there are currently no Grumman-*built* Wildcats flying, but that may change as several F4Fs in very reasonable condition have been recovered from Lake Michigan (however, experienced restorer and pilot Roy Stafford has stated, 'they may look good – the paint intact and the aluminum decent, but the steel and iron parts are probably all shot') where they 'went over the side' of the Navy's two lake-bound paddle-wheel training carriers. Certainly one of the most flown Wildcats is the FM-2P operated by Howard Pardue. In this view, accompanied by the Confederate Air Force's FM-2, the camera ports are clearly visible in the bottom of the fuselage. FM-2P (BuNo 86777) N5HP (ex-N90541) was obtained in less than ideal condition by Howard Pardue from Junior Burchinal in Paris, Texas, where it was returning back to 'Mother Nature', having swapped its engine to keep Burchinal's B-17G in marginally flyable condition

Right As the early morning sun rises through a fog layer near N5HP's home base at Stephens County Airport, Breckenridge, Texas, Pardue displays the classic lines of the FM-2P for the camera. A small number of FM-2s were converted to the armed photo-recce role by the addition of cameras in the rear lower fuselage. The original Grumman XF4F-1 started out life as a prototype biplane that would take over from where the classic F3F left off

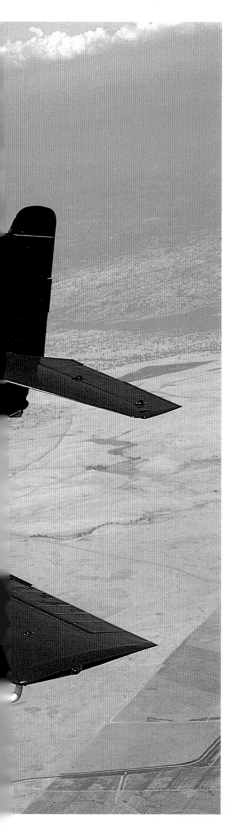

Above During the 1950s, most warbird-type aircraft were a shunned lot, often being banned from operating out of larger airfields. This rare view shows FM-2 (BuNo 86960) N18PK being run up at a farm airfield near La Grange, Illinois, by E J Saviano during October 1958. At this time, the monetary value of the Wildcat was extremely low – probably less than $2000 – and only a few somewhat eccentric individuals wished to operate the type

Left Pardue and the Wildcat high over California's central valley. Howard and his stable of aircraft regularly tour the warbird airshow circuit, and he puts on magnificent aerobatic displays in the Wildcat, Corsair, Bearcat and Hawker Fury fitted with a thundering Wright R-3350 radial. The Wright R-1820 on the Wildcat is a later variant and offers a bit more horsepower than the original F4F powerplant. The initial XF4F-2 had two .50 calibre Browning machine guns in the upper cowling and could carry two 100 lb bombs under the wing. A fly-off competition held in 1939 between the Wildcat and the Brewster F2A Buffalo saw the Buffalo chosen as the new Navy fighter – a mistake that would cost many USN/USMC and Allied pilots their lives. However, a follow-up order for a modified Wildcat meant that America would enter World War 2 on 7 December 1941, with an eminently usable, if not exactly high-tech, naval fighter

Above After the war, not many Wildcats survived the mass scrappings, but the handful that did led curious lives. A few were retained for 'sport' flying but the majority were put to work, with most being modified as agricultural (Ag) sprayers; huge drop tanks filled with chemicals were hung from the bomb pylons and dispersing bars were mounted under the wing. With these modifications, Wildcats could cover large swaths of acreage. FM-2 (BuNo 74560) N90253 is seen in less than ideal condition during the late 1960s. This aircraft eventually passed to the Champlin Fighter Museum, Mesa, Arizona, where it is maintained in airworthy condition but is unfortunately not flown

Right By May 1983, the CAF's Wildcat had been completely rebuilt and is seen near Breckenridge, Texas, in the colourful pre-war markings of VF-41 'Black Aces' operating off the USS *Ranger*. During August 1939, the US Navy placed orders for 54 F4F-3 Wildcats – an important milestone for the fighter that would eventually hinder Japanese aggression in the Pacific

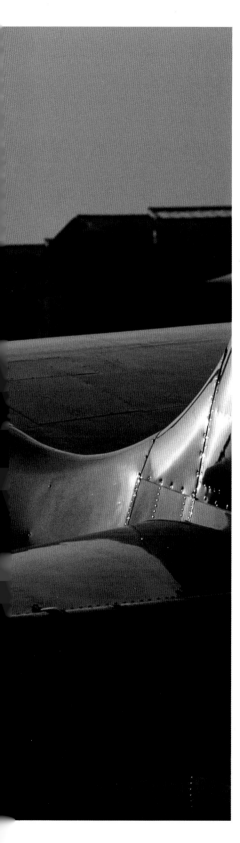

Above During the 1950s, one of the very few individuals that cared for the preservation of vintage and veteran aircraft was Ed Maloney and his developing air museum. Maloney managed to rescue two Wildcats — one flyable, one static. The flyable example is FM-2 (BuNo 55627) N7906C which is seen, with its registration painted out, at Chino, California, during November 1973 — a time when The Air Museum was facing financial difficulties. N7906C was sold to James Nunn, an airline pilot, who went on to restore the fighter under the new registration N47201. By 1982, the Wildcat had transferred to Stephen Grey. Also during the 1980s, Nunn and his co-pilot were shot to death aboard a PSA BAe 146 by a crazed airline employee. The airliner plunged into California hill country, killing all on board

Left During June 1982, ferry pilot John Crocker flew FM-2 N47201 to Britain, suffering a massive engine failure just after landing in Iceland; what would have happened a half hour earlier? The aircraft was based at Duxford with Grey, but did not participate in many shows before being sold to Bob Pond in 1986. The late afternoon sun highlights the simple but rugged construction of the fighter, photographed at Duxford in May 1985

Above Everything down and out, Lex Dupont puts FM-2 (BuNo 47030) N315E in the carrier landing configuration over Hamilton, Ontario, Canada, during June 1985. A very stock aircraft, N315E still retains its tail hook. Eastern built 1060 FM-1s, which were basically similar to the F4F-4. The FM-2 was Eastern's version of the XF4F-8 with a taller vertical tail, R-1820-56A Wright engine, more fuel, and greater underwing armament capacity. Eastern built 4777 FM-2s

Left The Wildcat was an extremely effective fighter for the Royal Navy – Fleet Air Arm Martlets (the rather unattractive name bestowed on the type by the British) scored several victories over *Luftwaffe* aircraft during the early years of the war. N47201 is seen parked with other veteran warriors at Duxford before its return to the States. In order to increase the flow of Wildcats reaching Allied squadrons, a licensing contract was established with the Eastern Aircraft Division of General Motors in Linden, New Jersey

Above They also serve. This ruin of an FM-2 was recovered from a lake bottom where it had sat for over four decades. Seen in the yard of the Yankee Air Corps Museum at Chino, the hulk of this Wildcat provided useful parts for the two Wildcats undergoing restoration at the museum

Left FM-2 N315E displays its aerobatic prowess. The Royal Navy received 370 FM-2s designated Wildcat VIs (fortunately, the Martlet name had been dropped by this stage). Currently, around a dozen Wildcats are flyable, five are undergoing restoration and another 14 are on display in museums

Above left Certainly one of the most unusual Wildcats still flying is FM-2 (BuNo 86680) (ex NX5558, N777A, YV-T-OTO, YV-T-HTJ). Somewhere along the line, the spacious interior of this Wildcat was modified to a 'cabin class' fitment with seats and windows for additional passengers (we wonder about the centre of gravity!). Currently owned by Dick Foote, the Wildcat is seen on a May 1984 outing over the Banana River in Florida with Foote at the controls

Left Dick Foote taxies FM-2, N11FE at Titusville, Florida, during March 1985. The windows, door, and porthole (!) for the passengers in the rotund fuselage can be clearly seen

Above Dick Foote flying FM-2 N11FE with the Space Shuttle assembly building in the distant background. Of note are the non-standard tyres that don't exactly fit into the wheel wells. Foote, a Navy pilot, was sent to the Aleutians during World War 2 to fly Curtiss P-36s for the Army against the Japanese invaders — not exactly an enviable job. The aircraft is painted in the markings of a Wildcat operating from the USS *Tulage*. On 29 June 1975, previous owner Frederick Edison crashed the Wildcat into Lake Michigan (site of so many wartime Wildcat crashes) while making a low pass. Fortunately, the aircraft suffered only minor damage and was raised from the lake bottom and rebuilt

Although the insignia on the wing in the lower right corner might appear rather ominous, the situation is benign since the Japanese *hinomaru* is affixed to the wing of Howard Pardue's AT-6D Texan, which was being utilized as a 'camera-ship' during May 1987 when photographing John Hooper's FM-2 (BuNo 47160) N551TC (ex-N2876D) over Breckenridge, Texas. Wildcat production totalled 7825 aircraft including 1988 Grumman F4Fs built between September 1937 and May 1943. Eastern contributed 5837 FMs between August 1942 and August 1945

Above Getting two Wildcats in the same place at the same time is not an overly common occurrence so it was with pleasure that we were able to record Howard Pardue in formation with John Hooper in N551TC. In the break, the deep recess for the camera port on Pardue's FM-2P N5HP can be clearly seen. During the war, Britain operated no less than 1123 Martlets/Wildcats, being the largest foreign operator of the type

Right John Hooper breaks away from the AT-6D in N551TC *Old Fang*, illustrating to advantage the retracted landing gear – a curious hand-cranked system favoured by Grumman. Also visible are the openings for ejecting spent .50 calibre shells and the closed over windows behind the main gear that had allowed the pilot a downward view. N551TC started its civil life as an agricultural aircraft with Western Aerial Contractors in Eugene, Oregon

Above Fresh from an in-depth total restoration by the Yankee Air Corps Museum, Chuck Hall positions FM-2 (BuNo 86819) N5833 over the hills near San Diego, California, during December 1987. This aircraft had been operated as a crop sprayer with Butler Aviation in Redmond, Oregon, before being damaged in a landing accident and stored. The FM-2 passed through several owners with little work being done on it until acquisition by the Yankee Air Corps Museum in 1981

Right FM-2 N5833 displays its classic lines near San Diego. The Wildcat is now owned by the Confederate Air Force's Air Group One and the aircraft made its first post-restoration flight on 24 April 1987

Above left Gear down, Chuck Hall flies downwind for finals at Ramona, California, in FM-2 N5833. Supported by an enthusiastic group of volunteers, the rare fighter is maintained in excellent condition. Note the stainless steel panel around the Wright's exhaust

Left Wearing 'sea search' style World War 2 camouflage, FM-2 (BuNo 86581) N1PP (ex-N86581) is seen at the annual Experimental Aircraft Association (EAA) Convention at Oshkosh, Wisconsin, during 1974. Currently, this aircraft is owned and operated by the Kalamazoo Aviation History Museum in Michigan

Above With its wings folded, FM-2 (BuNo 86690) N20HA displays its compact lines. N20HA operated with Don Underwood in Phoenix, Arizona, during the 1950s as a sprayer. The aircraft passed through several owners and went into storage until being obtained by Lenhardt Airpark in Hubbard, Oregon, and restored back into flying condition. The Wildcat is seen at Merced, California, on 1 June 1974. The FM-2 was donated to the Naval Aviation Museum during 1978

Above FM-2 (BuNo 86747) N68843 had been stored for many years in Tonapah, Nevada, by C T 'Red' Jensen, a long-time crop duster. After Jensen's death, the Wildcat passed to Kenneth Spiva who restored the aircraft back to flying condition. The FM-2 is seen at the September 1974 Gathering of Warbirds, held at Chandler Field, Fresno, California. This display was one of the very first fly-ins organized as a salute to restored World War 2 aircraft. N68843, like N20HA in the foreground, was eventually donated to the Naval Aviation Museum

Right FM-2 (BuNo 86774) N7835C is the Wildcat that remains in The Air Museum collection at Chino. This aircraft had been housed at a technical school near today's Los Angeles International Airport for many years, the school's close proximity to the coast, and the associated salt air, causing extensive corrosion to the airframe before being rescued by Ed Maloney. Today, the Wildcat is a static display at Chino, but given the talent and resources of the museum, N7835C may well fly once again

F6F Hellcat

The Grumman F6F Hellcat is one of the most successful naval aircraft of all time, yet it has been generally neglected by historians. The Hellcat, in just under two years of combat, achieved an unsurpassed victory ratio over the enemy as F6F pilots accounted for 55 per cent of all enemy aircraft destroyed by the USN/USMC during World War 2. Pilots were credited with 5156 victories over enemy aircraft with a loss of 270 Hellcats. Today, the Hellcat is a very rare aircraft with only a half dozen airworthy examples still regularly flying, while a few more are under restoration and around a dozen are displayed in museums. F6F-5 (BuNo 93879) N4994V is owned and flown by The Air Museum and is seen here in formation with the museum's Douglas SBD-5 Dauntless during a May 1989 outing

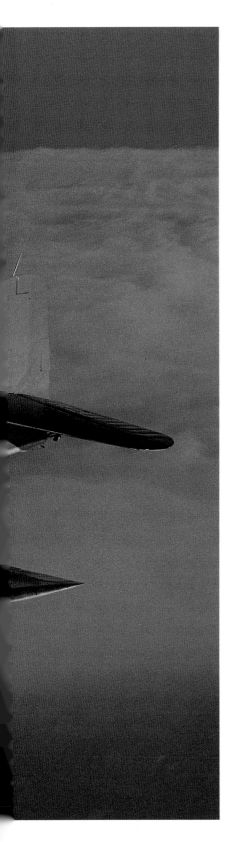

Above Certainly not one of the most attractive fighter aircraft of the period, the Hellcat's purposeful lines do, however, illustrate why it was such an effective warplane. Design 35 evolved into Design 50 and the Navy gave Grumman a free hand to create a fighter that could replace the new Chance Vought F4U Corsair in case problems developed with that design. Grumman engineers opted for a rugged fighter that would be highly carrier compatible (the Corsair had serious shortcomings revealed during carrier testing) and easy to produce. The Navy ordered two XF6F-1 prototypes on 30 June 1941, which was also the same day that the Corsair was ordered into production

Left One of the most regularly flown aircraft in The Air Museum collection, N4994V is seen above a light cloud deck over Burbank, California, during November 1988 with Mike DeMarino at the controls. Grumman Design 35 took two previous design concepts for an improved Wildcat and combined the best features to create a new fighter aircraft that would be powered by a Wright R-2600 radial. Design work can be traced back to 1938, but work on the new fighter was temporarily suspended to develop the XF4F-3 after the Navy's decision to purchase the Brewster F2A Buffalo

Over the years, the Confederate Air Force has operated two Hellcats. F6F-5 (BuNo 94385) N7861C was written off at Victoria, Texas, during July 1969, whilst the second example, F6F-5N BuNo 80166 was discovered derelict at Fergus Falls, Minnesota, during 1962 by John Sandberg, who purchased the aircraft and then meticulously restored it back to flying condition as N1078Z. In 1972, John donated the aircraft to the CAF where it flies regularly. The first XF6F-1 flew on 26 June 1942 and was the only Wright-powered example of the Hellcat to fly since a decision had been made early on in the programme to fit all production aircraft with the more powerful Pratt & Whitney R-2800 radial

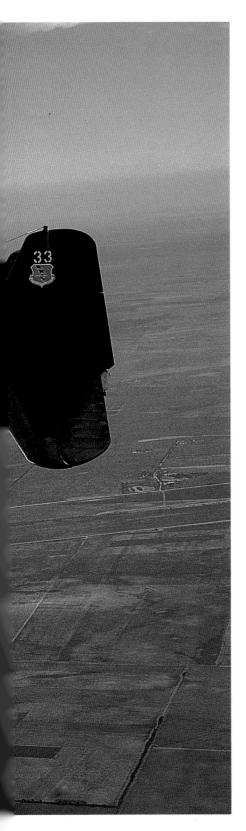

Above One of the stranger 'catches' trawled from the sea was this F6F-5 (BuNo 66237), recovered by the Navy from 3400 feet of water off the coast of San Diego, California. The aircraft was raised from the sea bottom on 9 October 1970 in an elaborate operation that illustrated the Navy's deep sea recovery capabilities to advantage. The fighter had been ditched following engine trouble on 12 January 1944 and the pilot successfully escaped from the sinking fighter. Currently, the Hellcat is displayed as found at the Pima Air Museum in Tucson, Arizona. The lack of vegetation and oxygen at that depth kept the airframe in remarkably good condition, and much of the equipment functioned after cleaning – even the Browning .50 calibre machine guns

Left N1078Z passes under the wing of the B-25 'camera-ship'. Over the years, this aircraft has worn a number of paint schemes including its post-restoration gloss overall black with a red stripe. Since the need for new fighters was so great, the Navy placed orders for 1080 Hellcats five months before the prototype flew and Grumman would go on to build 12,275 F6Fs at its Bethpage plant

Above With its wings folded, N4998V makes a fairly compact package on the Lone Star ramp in Galveston. As can be seen, the aircraft was very heavily detailed during its 2½-year restoration by Steve Picatti. BuNo 94204 was accepted by the Navy on 27 July 1945 but remained in storage for a good deal of its service life. When all remaining Hellcats were declared surplus on 9 July 1957, '204 had only 603 flying hours on the airframe and 303 hours on the overhauled R-2800. After Maloney traded the Hellcat (one of two he obtained from a scrap company) to Eddie Fisher for a Heinkel He-162, Fisher's plans to restore and fly the F6F did not come to fruition and the fighter was sold to Coutches in May 1970. After performing some work on the aircraft, Coutches flew it to Hayward

Left The scoreboard on this beautifully restored and detailed Hellcat reflects the impressive victory tally of US Navy ace Alex Vraciu. Owned and operated by the Lone Star Flight Museum, F6F-5N (BuNo 94204) N4998V was surplused during 1959 and was acquired by The Air Museum's Ed Maloney. The aircraft was eventually sold to Michael Coutches of Hayward, California, and put into storage along with another Hellcat he owned

Above This is how BuNo 94204 looked in July 1967 when the museum was housed at Ontario Airport. As can be seen, the aircraft is completely stock and still in its original paint, complete with the name *The Bequine* on the forward fuselage. The aircraft was rolled out of Picatti's shop on 24 February 1989, and was taxied under its own power for the admiring spectators, among whom was Alex Vraciu, who proudly viewed the aircraft finished in his markings when he flew with VF-16 'Airdales'. Vraciu scored 19 victories against the Japanese, becoming the Navy's fourth-ranking ace. However, Vraciu was also known as Grumman's 'best customer' since he had two carriers sunk under him, baled out of one Hellcat and ditched two other F6Fs in the ocean (one due to combat damage, the other to engine failure)

Right Ed Vesly flying Lone Star's Hellcat during May 1990. The first post-restoration flight took place on 4 May 1989 with Glenn MacDonald at the controls. Alex Vraciu had an impressive combat record that included the downing of six Yokosuka D4Y2 *Judy* dive bombers in just eight minutes while expending only 360 of the 2400 rounds of .50 calibre carried in the Hellcat's gun bays. This event took place on 19 June 1944 during the famous battle that was to become known as the 'Marianas Turkey Shoot'

Above left F6F-3 (BuNo 08825) N4965V on the ramp at Chandler Field, Fresno, during September 1974. The oldest of the surviving Hellcats, this aircraft is owned by Willard Compton who crashed it while attempting to land at his small farm strip in Canby, Oregon, on 12 June 1977. Compton was severly injured but survived, and the Hellcat was badly damaged and placed in storage. Over the years, Compton has gathered many Hellcat spare parts and a rebuild is not out of the question. The first major production variant of the Hellcat was the F6F-3 and the first example was flown by Bob Hall on 30 July 1942. Grumman built 4402 -3 Hellcats and 500 aircraft were being delivered each month by February 1944

Left This abandoned Hellcat is seen at Chicagoland Airport, Illinois, during July 1974 when it was in distinctly less than pristine condition. Note how the skinning has been removed from the lower wing. F6F-5K (BuNo 79683) N7896C was apparently to be used as a high-altitude mapping aircraft but it is not known if this mission was ever undertaken before the aircraft finally became derelict. Fortunately, the Hellcat was purchased in 1981 by the Kalamazoo Aviation History Museum and removed to their headquarters for total restoration

Above When Kalamazoo received their Hellcat, they completely broke the aircraft apart and began a ground-up restoration that retured the rare fighter to better than new condition. When the fighter was ready for flight, the new registration N4PP was applied and as can be seen, the Hellcat looks magnificent in its overall glossy sea blue camouflage finish with insignia white markings

Boring a hole through the smoggy air near Chino, Mike DeMarino flies wing in The Air Museum's Hellcat on Bob Pond's freshly-finished F6F-5K (BuNo 94473) N4964W during a May 1984 photo flight. Pond, a World War 2 Naval Aviator, has collected a wide variety of vintage aircraft at his Planes of Fame East Museum in Minnesota. This Hellcat had been with The Air Museum for many years until it was purchased by Pond and passed to Steve Hinton's Fighter Rebuilders for restoration to flying status. Grumman built a total of 7868 F6F-5s and the -5K variant came about in 1949 when quite a few Hellcats were converted to target drones. Naturally, most of these fine aircraft were expended in this mission due to the nature of testing, but some did survive to help bolster today's F6F population. The conversion programme continued until 1957

Above Bob Pond's Hellcat is seen taxying for take-off at Titusville, Florida, during March 1985 at the big Valiant Air Command airshow which kicks off the yearly round of warbird events. As we go to press, restorer Roy Stafford has recovered over half a dozen damaged F6F-5K airframes from San Nicholas Island off the California coast where the Navy has a large drone base. It is hoped that at least one of the aircraft can be rebuilt into a flyer

Left A rather well-worn BuNo 94473 is seen at The Air Museum in Ontario during September 1965. It appears that the aircraft suffered some form of landing or take-off accident and the Hellcat still wears the majority of its drone colour scheme, although the left wing may be a replacement since it is finished in a utility scheme often worn by drone 'directors' (F6F-5D). Once again, it was through Ed Maloney's dedication that this aircraft, certainly fit for the scrap heap by early 1960s' standards, was saved to fly once again

Above The Navy's China Lake base in the hostile California desert has seen many unusual weapon experiments over the years and quite a few of these experiments have involved former World War 2 aircraft as targets. F6F-5K BuNo 79192 is seen in the base's storage yard after being retrieved from a target range where it had been mounted upside down for many years to test a variety of explosives. When photographed during June 1971, the Hellcat was up for disposal and was apparently transferred to the Bradley Air Museum in Windsor Locks, Connecticut, during 1976. Several wrecks are still on the China Lake range and may eventually yield a few more parts for other restorations

Right Of the small number of Hellcats on the civil register, two have been extensively damaged in crashes – the aforementioned N4965V and F6F-5K (BuNo 80141) N100TF which was owned by Tom Friedkin and being flown by Bill Yoak when engine problems caused a crash landing near San Marcos, California, on 3 April 1979. The aircraft hit a ditch and was very heavily damaged as can be seen in this photo, which was taken shortly after the accident when the F6F had been trucked back to its home base at Palomar Airport. A fuselage which had been in a small museum in Illinois was eventually obtained and other parts were gathered to attempt a rebuild but the Hellcat was eventually sold to the Yankee Air Corps in 1983 and a rebuild back to flying condition was, amazingly, completed and N100FT once again took to the air. Examination of the replacement fuselage showed that the aircraft had infact been the personal mount of Navy ace Alex Vraciu! In 1989, the Hellcat was sold to Stephen Grey's The Fighter Collection, Duxford, England. When the F6F arrived in the UK it was painted in Vraciu's markings so out of the small population of surviving Hellcats, two are finished in the ace's colours

F7F Tigercat

Above Certainly one of the most aggressive looking of all World War 2 fighter designs, the Grumman F7F Tigercat missed out on combat as the first operational squadron landed in Okinawa on the last day of the war. Jim Fausz is seen flying F7F-3 (BuNo 80503) N800RW over Breckenridge, Texas, during May 1990. During June 1941, Grumman was awarded two contracts to build a large twin-engine fighter – one was from the Army Air Corps for the XP-65 and the other was from the Navy for two XF7F-1 prototypes. Grumman Design 51 was for an advanced fighter, the Army model having a pressurized cockpit while the Navy aircraft would be unpressurized

Right The Army dropped out of the XP-65 programme in order to let Grumman concentrate on its Naval project. The XF7F-1 was designed to operate from the new *Midway*-class carriers and from land bases. The design was changed a number of times and progress was slow at best since military priority was being given to F6F Hellcat production. The Pratt & Whitney R-2800 was chosen for power. In this view, F7F-3P (BuNo 80425) N7235C is seen waiting for its next mission at Sequoia Field, California, during march 1973, while the wings in the foreground are also off a Tigercat. TBM Inc., operators of the Tigercat, kept a spare, non-civilianized airframe for parts and it was this aircraft that was purchased and restored by the Lone Star Flight Museum, Galveston, Texas, as N800RW. Fifty-eight F7F-3s were modifed to -3P photo recce specs by the Lockheed Modification Center at Van Nuys, in California, during 1945

Above After Lone Star purchased the disassembled Tigercat, the airframe was shipped to Fort Collins, Colorado, for a ground-up restoration and the result was a magnificent example of the rebuilder's art. The finely-finished F7F-3 is seen on the ramp at the Lone Star's Galveston museum on 13 November 1990. The Tigercat was armed with four nose-mounted .50 calibre machine guns and four wing-mounted 20 mm cannon, giving the aircraft an awesome firepower. The first official flight for the XF7F-1 took place on 2 November 1943

Right The extremely narrow fuselage of the Tigercat was a concession to make the big aircraft as streamlined as possible. Early testing showed the F7F to be very powerful and manoeuvrable. From the start, the Navy wanted to utilize the single-seat aircraft as a night fighter and production aircraft were fitted with AN/APS-6 radar, thus becoming the first single-seat fighter with internal radar. Later night fighting variants were built as two-seaters

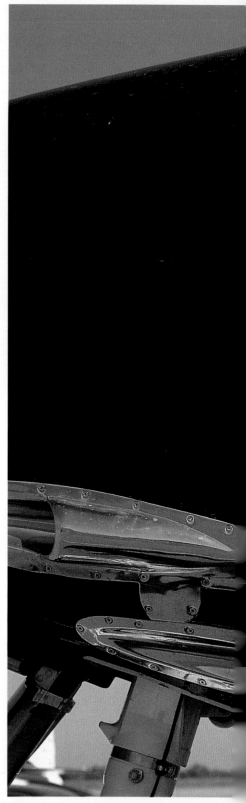

Above Lone Star's Tigercat is accompanied by the museum's Hellcat. N800RW is finished in an overall black colour scheme worn by some Tigercats flying with VMF(N)-513 'Flying Nightmares' during the Korean War. F7F-3Ns scored several victories over slow Po-2 biplanes that were used for night raids on American bases. The Tigercats also successfully took part in night close support missions against the enemy.

Right The attractive nose art on N800RW. Lone Star's F7F-3 is regularly flown to airshows around the country and holds the distinction of being the only flying Tigercat not to have been a fire bomber. Grumman built a total of 250 F7F-3s in three sub-variants

Above F7F-3 (BuNo 80532) N7195C awaits its next call for a hazardous fire bombing mission at Porterville, California, during September 1975 while being operated by Sis-Q. Note the companion B-17G Flying Fortress in the background – except for five PB4Y-2 Privateers, all former World War 2 combat aircraft have now been withdrawn from the fire bombing role in the United States. The big Tigercat had a tough time during carrier compatibility trials and the fighter never really fitted in with carrier operations so the majority of Tigercat missions were flown from land bases

Right N7195C became the first 'warbird' Tigercat when it was purchased by Gary Flanders and Mike Bogue during 1979, after being phased out of its fire bombing duties. Initially, the owners added a couple of stars and bars and took the F7F around to shows in its basic fire bomber colour scheme. Later, however, the fighter was stripped and a very authentic military paint scheme was applied. Gary Flanders is seen airborne over California's central valley in the F7F during August 1981. This view shows the second seat, which was originally occupied by the radar operator in the -3N, to advantage

Above As soon as surplus Tigercats became available, they were modified for other missions. One of the first F7Fs on the civil register was fitted with a smoke system and used for skywriting while another aircraft was fitted with underwing containers for fire bombing, but this set-up did not prove effective. However, during the 1950s an air tanker conversion for the Tigercat saw the fitting of a large 800 gallon container under the fuselage and the F7F became a very effective fire bomber. Fifteen Tigercats were eventually modified for the air attack role and were operated by Butler Aviation, TBM Inc, Sis-Q Flying Service, and Cal-Nat Airways. F7F-3 (BuNo 80525) N7238C is seen at the scenic Loma Rica Air Attack Base, Grass Valley, California, during September 1968 when it was being operated by Sis-Q. Tanker 22F was destroyed in a fatal crash at Rohnerville, California, on 21 October 1974

Above right A setting sun at Grass Valley outlines the sleek shape of F7F-3N (BuNo 80374) N7629C during September 1970. This aircraft was originally operated by Cal-Nat Airways before being sold to Sis-Q Flying Services. Pilots liked the F7F for aerial attack since the aircraft had good power reserves and was quite manoeuvrable, even with the large retardant tank. Although the initial Navy contract to Grumman called for 650 F7F-1s, the end of the war and cutbacks saw only 364 Tigercats of all variants built

Right N7629C during September 1974 when it had acquired the smart orange and white scheme applied to Sis-Q's Tigercats. The F7F-3 featured a larger vertical tail to help increase directional stability. All surviving Tigercats are -3 variants

Bob Forbes flying TBM Inc's F7F-3N (BuNo 80390) N6129C over the south Texas coast during October 1977. The 800 gallon tank has been removed, allowing the aircraft to display its sleek lines. This fighter was even entered in the Reno National Air Races and qualified, but was withdrawn from the formal competition. Forbes, a long-time tanker pilot, has flown just about every type of fire bomber and the Tigercat was one of his favourites. The retractable step did not retract on the photo flight, thus leaving one slight blemish to the aircraft's clean lines

Above When N6129C was withdrawn from service, tanker 62E passed to an owner in Knoxville, Tennessee, who registered the aircraft as N700FM and began restoration back to military configuration. However, the project was sold to the Kalamazoo Aviation History Museum who took over the restoration and brought the aircraft back to magnificent flying status as N700F. As with the majority of Kalamazoo's aircraft, the Tigercat is flown regularly. The F7F is finished in the markings of the USMC's VMO-254

Right Fortunately, fire bomber operators are a lot like 'pack rats' since they rarely throw anything away. F7F-3 (BuNo 80410) N7627C suffered a gear-up landing at Grass Valley while being operated by Cal-Nat Airways. At the time, it was not economically feasible to repair the aircraft, even though it was not that badly damaged, so the Tigercat was disassembled and stuffed behind one of the hangars where it served as a parts source. In the late 1980s, the fighter was purchased by Kermit Weeks, who has the F7F-3 in storage pending a possible rebuild to flying condition

Above F7F-3N (BuNo 80382) on display at The Air Museum, Chino, California. Put on display during 1991, this aircraft had been at NAS Anacostia for many years and was acquired by the USMC Museum in poor condition. The aircraft has been put into static display condition and still retains the original night fighter radar nose which is missing from other civilian -3Ns. An initial batch of 49 Tigercats was fitted to -3N standard at the Lockheed Modification Center with the addition of SCR-720 radar and the deletion of the four nose-mounted .50 calibre machine guns

Left F7F-3P (BuNo 80425) N7235C on the ramp at Chino, California, during May 1975. Former tanker 64E is now owned by the Military Aircraft Restoration Group, but is rarely flown. The fighter had previously been operated by Butler Aviation and TBM Inc

F8F Wildcat

Above Leroy Grumman was worried that his company's direction towards large twin-engined fighters like the XF7F was leaving a big gap when it came to smaller, more agile fighters that could operate off all the carrier classes used by the Navy. Grumman issued a memo to chief engineer Bill Schwendler during mid-July 1943 to create 'a small fighter plane, which could (without question) be used on large or small carriers, and with a performance superior to the F6F.' The result was Grumman Design 58 – the F8F Bearcat. One of the most attractive of all surviving Bearcats never actually saw military service – N700A was built up out of parts, stemming from a Grumman 21 July 1949 request to build such an aircraft for company use. Steve Hinton is seen piloting the fighter in this photograph

Right For his new fighter design, Leroy Grumman specified that he wanted an aircraft as small as the Wildcat, but fitted with a powerful Pratt & Whitney R-2800, four .50 machine guns, bubble canopy, wide track landing gear for better ground handling, and dazzling performance. Design 58 started with company funding, but the Navy liked what they saw and signed an order for two XF8F-1s on 27 November 1943 – the first prototype flew on 31 August 1944 with Robert Hall at the controls. Howard Pardue displays the compact lines of G-58B N700A over Chino, California, during May 1986 (the G-58A was a civil -1 built up for famed aerobatic pilot Al Williams. Named *Gulfhawk IV*, the aircraft was destroyed during a landing accident on 18 January 1949 at Newbury, North Carolina, Williams surviving the crash). The fighter was built up for one of aviation's more interesting personalities – Roger Wolfe Kahn – who, at the time, was Grumman's director of service and product support and wanted to utilize the speedy Bearcat to visit various naval bases across the country that were operating Grumman products

Above Over the barren San Bernardino Mountains, Howard Pardue tucks the G-58B close into the 'camera-ship'. In 1941, Kahn joined Grumman to organize and manage the company's service department. He was also a test pilot for Wildcats, Hellcats, and Avengers. However, in 1962, Kahn was struck with cancer and died at the early age of 54. With its useful life coming to an end, Leroy Grumman donated N700A to the Cornell Aeronautical Laboratory in Buffalo, New York. Cornell used the aircraft for some flight testing experiments but by 1966 the fighter had been sold on the civil market. In 1969 it was purchased by Bill Fornof for his dual Bearcat airshow act. In 1984, the F8F passed to the Champlin Fighter Museum, but it is now owned by Bob Pond's Planes of Fame East and is regularly flown

Left A rare gathering – Steve Hinton flies the G-58B while Howard Pardue breaks to the right in his XF8F-1. Roger Wolfe Kahn became a common sight in the Bearcat as he visited Navy units operating Panthers, Cougars and Tigers. A true aviation buff, Kahn was admired by everyone who knew him, and came from an extremely unusual background. Kahn's father was a very wealthy New York banker. Roger always loved music and organized his own dance band before he was 17. With the help of a $25,000 loan from his father, Kahn expanded his musical horizon to include eleven orchestras which were netting him a personal income of $50,000 a year by the time he was 18

Above Arguably one of the most attractive Bearcats painted in a civilian colour scheme was F8F-2P (BuNo 121608) N7700C owned and flown by J W 'Bill' Fornof of Houma, Louisiana. Fornof purchased the -2P in 1963 with a view of using the powerful fighter as an airshow mount. Finished in a striking scheme, Fornof became an adept airshow performer and even had a Mustang painted in a matching scheme. In military service, the -2P variant was fitted with a camera package in the fuselage and the wing armament was reduced to two 20 mm cannon. Sixty -2Ps were obtained for the armed photo recon role. Fornof's airshow act became so popular that he acquired G-58B N700A to form a dual aerobatic team with his son Corky. The team became very popular but tragedy struck on 5 June 1971 at NAS Quonset Point in Rhode Island when the wing of N7700C failed during an airshow (after the Bearcat, already under extreme stress, hit a micro-burst of wind shear) and the Bearcat snapped into the ground and exploded, killing Bill Fornof instantly

Left When Kahn received the G-58B, he was delighted and immediately began utilizing the fighter for Grumman's benefit. As a teenager, Kahn began taking flying lessons and quickly progressed. With his large income, he began buying aircraft by the time he was 19. His machines included a Bellanca monoplane modelled after the record-setting *Columbia* which Clarence Chamberlin flew from New York to Berlin. Other aircraft included a military Vought Corsair (the biplane), a highly modified Standard, and an Ireland amphibion. He kept his aircraft at Roosevelt Field and began palling around with the famous aviators of the time

Above During the 1960s, the few surviving Bearcats were scattered across the country and seldom flown, their resale value actually being less than the more popular North American P-51D Mustang. A typical example was F8F-2 (BuNo 121589) N5171V which is seen looking rather neglected at New Haven, Connecticut, on 15 August 1964. The aircraft was owned by Norwood Hanson, a college professor, who eventually disposed of the tatty paint in favour of an attractive airshow-style scheme and began flying an aerobatic routine in the fighter (changing the registration to N5555H) until he smacked into a mountain near Scott, New York, during 1969. The F8F-2 was created by the addition of a Pratt & Whitney R-2800-34W radial of 2250 hp and featured a simplified cowling and a taller vertical tail (increased by one foot) to enhance stability. Grumman built 293 F8F-2s and the aircraft were armed with four 20 mm cannon in the wing

Right Looking considerably worse for the wear, F8F-2 BuNo 121707 is seen returning back to nature after use by Kaman Helicopters as a wind machine. Kaman had obtained two surplus Bearcats from the Navy around 1959 and used the powerful P&Ws to generate wind-storms in order to test the ability of their various helicopters to withstand high winds. Since these aircraft were not going to fly again, Kaman simply tossed away the outer wing panels in order to reduce space. Little was done to maintain the aircraft, other than to make sure the engines were kept in running order. When photographed during August 1970, the Bearcat had outlived its usefulness with Kaman and was disposed of shortly afterwards, both airframes being obtained by the US Marine Corps Museum

Above The powerful and compact lines of F8F-2 (BuNo 122637) N198F are well-displayed in this view of the aircraft at Chino during May 1983. Attractively finished and well-maintained, the Bearcat is owned by Tom Friedkin of Palomar, California, and is only occasionally displayed at airshows. This particular aircraft became N1033B in 1963 and went through numerous owners before being acquired by Friedkin. Since this photograph was taken, a second seat has been installed behind the pilot. Because of its small size, the Navy found they could park 50 Bearcats on a carrier in the same space that would be taken by only 36 F6F Hellcats

Left BuNo 121707 was not fated to sit out its days in a dusty museum, however, the bedraggled airframe being involved in a trade to Wally McDonnell at Mojave, California, where the Bearcat is seen in his hanger during February 1976. Wally sold the fighter to Elmer Ward at Chino, California, who began a ground-up restoration and, as we go to press, the F8F is approaching its first flight. It appears that the civil registration N1027B was assigned to the Bearcat in the early 1960s, but was certainly never applied to the aircraft as it never flew. During restoration, Ward was able to obtain some parts and the registration and paperwork for F8F-2 N7701C and this number has been applied to the new restoration. Ward has extended the cockpit area of his aircraft (along with a longer canopy) to house a second seat. Also, a new set of outer wing panels had to be scratch-built for the Bearcat as the originals could not be found

Above Looking every inch the potent racing machine it could be, F8F-2P (BuNo 121787) N148F is seen at Mojave, California, during October 1973 at one of the several unlimited air races held at the remote ex-USMC field. Starting civil life as N6821D in 1963, the aircraft was obtained by Bud Fountain's Hawke Dusters, based at Modesto in California, and several modifications were made to the aircraft for racing. The anodized aluminium finish that Grumman carefully gave each of its Bearcats to prevent salt water corrosion was sanded off by Fountain's crew and the raw aluminium underneath was highly polished. The Bearcat can be an unforgiving aircraft and during a race on 20 October 1973, the Pratt & Whitney let go and an intense fire started in the engine's magnesium parts. The Bearcat does not have much in the way of a firewall and the flames immediately burst into the cockpit. The Bearcat fell as a fireball onto the desert floor, exploding on impact in front of the thousands of race fans

Right Looking rather forlorn, F8F-2 BuNo 121751 is seen on 5 April 1968 at Moseley Field outside of Phoenix, Arizona. At that time, the dirt field was home to over half a dozen abandoned Corsairs, a crash-landed Mustang and a variety of other unusual aircraft, so the Bearcat fitted right in. N9885C was purchased in 1963 by William Stead of Reno and was in basically stock military condition. Stead single-handedly brought unlimited air racing back to the United States when he staged the first National Air Race in Reno during 1964. Sadly, Stead was killed in the crash of a Formula One racer and did not live to see the tremendous success of today's annual Reno events. N9885C was sold by his estate and went through several owners, including the irrepressible Junior Burchinal who offered instruction in the aircraft from his rudimentary airstrip in Paris, Texas. The fighter was one of several Bearcats eventually acquired by Harold 'Bubba' Beal and Charles 'Chubb' Smith of Knoxville, Tennessee. Smith flew the 'Cat into a thunderstorm on 18 June 1980 and was killed when the aircraft crashed near Commerce, Georgia

Above F8F-2 (BuNo 122629) N777L is Lyle Shelton's famous Wright R-3350 powered racer *Rare Bear*. This Bearcat has had so many modifications and markings changes that it could fill the entire Bearcat chapter in this book! We settled on this view of Lyle taxying out at Reno during the September 1987 event to show the powerful lines of what may be an unbeatable racer. The aircraft originally started out in civilian life as N1031B, but was almost immediately written off during a landing accident while being delivered to the owner at Valparaiso, Indiana. Lyle obtained the remains in 1968 and eventually built the aircraft into one of the most potent of all racers; the fighter currently holds the world's propeller-driven aircraft speed record

Left Two XF8Fs were built along with a development batch of 23 aircraft, which are usually also referred to as XF8F-1s. These aircraft helped get the Bearcat ready for operations and on 21 May 1945, F8F-1s were delivered to VF-19 – less than nine months after the first XF8F had flown. For some reason, XF8F-1 BuNo 90446 was saved from scrapping and placed in store with what would become known as the National Air and Space Museum. In this August 1970 view, the aircraft is seen in poor condition in outside storage at the museum's Silver Hill facility. Eventually deemed of little interest to the museum since it was a prototype aircraft, the XF8F-1 was traded to Darryl Greenamyer (along with several other aircraft) as a spares source for his record-holding F8F-2 N1111L during 1976. Greenamyer soon sold the aircraft to George Enhorning, who registered the Bearcat N99279 and began an extensive restoration. A magnificently finished Bearcat was eventually rolled out of the Wolcott Air Service hangar in Connecticut, but several engine failures convinced Enhorning to sell the aircraft and the fighter passed to Howard Pardue in 1983 as N14HP

Howard Pardue's XF8F-1 is the world's most flown Bearcat since he regularly attends airshows and air races in N14HP. The Bearcat is seen in formation with other World War 2 classics over Houston, Texas, during September 1986. The Bearcat was rushed into service, and although VF-19 was heading for the combat zone Japan surrendered and the F8F failed to see action during the war. Although the Bearcat would go on to equip 32 squadrons during the late 1940s, orders for the type were drastically cut back due to the cessation of hostilities

Above Two of Grumman's best in formation: Pardue in the XF8F-1 is followed by the Confederate Air Force's FM-2 Wildcat. The Bearcat was stressed to a then impressive 7.5 positive Gs and 3.7 negative Gs, letting the pilots of the type outperform just about any other service fighter of the time. When the Korean War began during 1950, the Navy decided not to send the F8F into action because the Bearcat was not as efficient as the Corsair in the ground attack role

Right The fighters built by Grumman were some of the most rugged wartime aircraft to see service, yet they were also finely detailed as can be seen in this view of the XF8F-1, which also illustrates the ejector stacks for the P&W R-2800 radial engine

Howard Pardue has fitted his rare Bearcat with a smoke system for airshow work and he puts on a high-spirited show with the tight-turning XF8F. Some stability problems with the F8F-1 led to Grumman heightening the tail fin by one foot, resulting (along with other minor changes) in the next variant of the Bearcat, the F8F-2

Above With the rapid increase in unlimited air racing during the 1960s and 1970s, it was not unsurprising that the few surviving Bearcats were soon battling around the pylons with Mustangs and Corsairs. Finished in an attractive two-tone blue paint scheme, F8F-2 (BuNo 121748) N5005 is seen on the ramp at Stead Field in Reno during the September 1970 Reno National Air Race. This aircraft was originally surplused as N1028B and passed through several owners before being acquired by Chester Christopher in 1966 as N500B. TWA pilots Ron Reynolds and Mike Geren acquired the fighter in 1970 and began to attend air races with N5005. The heavy exhaust streaks on the fuselage indicate that the P&W was being run at high power settings

Right N5005 was entered in the US Cup Race at Brown Field, San Diego, California, during July 1971. This race was unlike Reno since it was a 1000-kilometre event which meant that some of the aircraft would have to land, refuel, and take-off again to join the race. Mike Geren (in the orange flight suit) is seen preparing to get into the cockpit during a refuelling stop. After rejoining the race with replenished tanks, the P&W came apart in the air and an intense fire entered the cockpit. The Bearcat fell blazing out of the sky and exploded on impact, killing the pilot

Above Basically stock F8F-2 (BuNo 122619), N7958C is seen at Chino during August 1973. Surplused from NAS Litchfield Park during 1963, the aircraft passed through several owners before it became one of three Bearcats owned by the Confederate Air Force. In 1973, the fighter was flown to Chino under the new ownership of Harold Beale and Charles Smith for an extensive rebuild. At the time, it was decided to make the F8F the finest Bearcat flying and a complete reconstruction of the airframe was undertaken with many parts being either chromed or anodized, resulting in it being nicknamed 'Chrome Cat'. The registration was changed to N700F and by 1978, the Bearcat was owned by Don Whittington as N14WB. Today, the F8F is on display at the EAA Museum in Oshkosh, Wisconsin

Right Of the three Bearcats originally operated by the Confederate Air Force, one was sold, one was crashed after the pilot apparently ran the aircraft out of fuel, and one was recently reflown after sitting idle at Chino for over six years. F8F-2 (BuNo 122674) N7825C was surplused in 1963 and went through several owners before being donated to the CAF in 1972. The aircraft had never really been completely restored and was eventually sent to Fighter Rebuilders. However, because of funding problems, Fighter Rebuilders basically did an engine change and an annual inspection. The aircraft is seen on 3 December 1991 prior to a test flight by Steve Hinton. As a point of interest, Hinton now owns the wreck of ex-CAF F8F-2 (BuNo 121614) N7957C and had started restoration to flying status in early 1992

Above F8F-2 (BuNo 122708) N7701C is seen at Norwalk, Connecticut, during February 1970 and is typical of the Bearcats of that period. N7701C is finished in an attractive civilian colour scheme and appears to be basically stock, down to the large roll-over structure behind the pilot. Surplused in 1963, the aircraft was one of the few Bearcats to survive the final scrappings at Litchfield Park. If there had been more civilian interest, more F8Fs would have survived, but the majority of the final batch of stored F8Fs was simply fed into the furnace. With cutbacks due to the end of the war, Grumman produced only 373 -2s including all different sub-variants. The Navy's precision display team the Blue Angels, flew Bearcats from 1946 to 1949

Right One of the most famous of all Bearcats is F8F-2 (BuNo 121646) N1111L (ex-N7699C) that was raced so successfully at Reno for many years by Lockheed test pilot Darryl Greenamyer. Considerably modified over the years (with the able assistance of Bruce Boland, Ray Poe and other volunteers), the Bearcat became a regular Reno winner and finally broke the ultimate propeller-driven speed record set by the Germans in 1939 during August 1969, when Greenamyer recorded a top speed of 483.041 mph over a measured course. After the aircraft was retired, it went to the National Air and Space Museum where it was displayed in the main facility, but the fighter is now in storage at Silver Hill. Greenamyer is seen running up the modified R-2800 at Mojave during June 1975

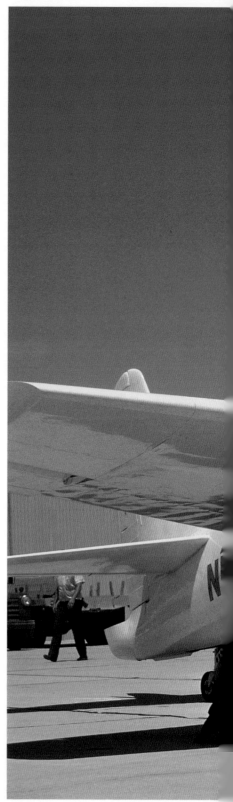

Left During 1973, N7701C was purchased by Jack Sliker of Wadley, Georgia. Sliker already owned a P-51D that he used for air racing and he had similar plans for the Bearcat. Sliker is seen running up the R-2800 at Mojave during June 1975. Note the racing modifications including spinner, clipped wings, and the removal of roll-over structure. While returning home from California on 16 September 1975, Sliker apparently ran the Bearcat out of fuel while on final approach to the airport at Flagstaff, Arizona, and was killed in the resulting crash. The remains of this aircraft, along with the paperwork, went to Elmer Ward for his Bearcat rebuild project.

Above The smaller vertical tail is readily apparent in this view of XF8F-1 (BuNo 90454) N9G seen at the September 1970 Reno National Air Races. Finished in a very distinctive colour scheme, this aircraft was originally acquired in 1959 by E D Weiner, one of the first warbird collector/operators, as N3351. Race pilot Gunther Balz acquired the F8F in 1968 and raced the Bearcat several times before retiring from air racing altogether

Above XF8F-1 N9G was eventually repainted in a Royal Thai Air Force scheme, but this was replaced after the Kalamazoo Aviation History Museum (who acquired the fighter in 1978) overhauled the aircraft and finished the Bearcat in accurate US Navy period markings. Around 150 F8F-1 Bearcats were supplied to the French *Armee de l'Air* for combat use in Indochina. When the French finally lost the war in 1954, surviving Bearcats were supplied to South Vietnam and Thailand, where the last flying example was not withdrawn until 1963. The Bearcats saw heavy combat against the forces of the Viet Minh

Right Detail view of N9G showing the squadron insignia, and the overall immaculate condition of the fighter that is typical of the aircraft operated by the Kalamazoo Aviation History Museum

Above Originally surplused as N1029B in 1963, F8F-2 BuNo 121748 became N618F around 1967 and acquired this distinctive 'great pumpkin' paint scheme. The aircraft went through several owners before being acquired by Harold Beal and Charles Smith, who began restoring the F8F back in to pristine condition as N200N. The Bearcat was then acquired by Don Whittington in 1982

Above right Certainly one of the least attractive paint schemes applied to a Bearcat was this one seen on F8F-2 (BuNo 122637) N1033B at the Reno National Air Races during September 1969 when it was owned by Dr Sherman Cooper. This aircraft later became N198F, which is illustrated elsewhere in this chapter

Right One of the more unusual tasks thrust upon a civil Bearcat (yet not totally unlike its -2P military role) was that of a high-altitude photo-mapping platform. F8F-2 (BuNo 121528) N212KA (ex-N9886C) was operated by Kucera and Associates, Cleveland, Ohio, after being surplused by the Navy. The company was a photo-mapping business and N212KA was suitably modified to house an operators seat in the spacious rear fuselage, along with an entry door and associated ports for camera equipment, which must have made for an interesting centre of gravity. Kucera entered the aircraft in several Reno events as racer 99 but the fighter was fairly unsuccessful due to its increased weight and lack of any race modifications. N212KA is seen being readied for the start of a race at the 1968 Reno event. The F8F crashed while landing at Lost Nations Airport in Ohio on 13 December 1968 and Kucera was killed

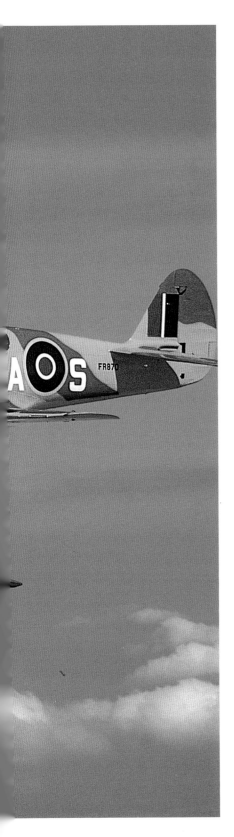

Above Ed Maloney's The Air Museum acquired military stock F8F-2P BuNo 121714 from the US Navy in the late 1950s. Although dilapidated, the aircraft was still in original markings (except for the addition of civilian registration N4995V) when photographed at Ontario Airport, California, during August 1967. The fighter was eventually moved to the museum's new permanent facility at Chino but, during a financial squeeze, the aircraft was sold to raise funds to keep the museum going. The new buyer was Harold Beal and Charles Smith who registered the aircraft as N1YY, although it is not known if this was ever taken up. The F8F was restored back to flying condition in the early 1970s with the registration N700H

Left Howard Pardue is seen flying N700H while Stephen Grey flies wing in his Curtiss Kittyhawk N1009N. Stephen Grey purchased N700H for his growing collection of vintage fighters during 1982 and had the Bearcat flown to his Duxford, England, base where it has operated successfully for many years

Above Pardue takes the Bearcat down low over lush farm fields prior to a high speed pass down the Duxford runway. N700H was joined in 1991 by F8F-2 (BuNo 121752) N800H (ex-N7827C and N2YY) which was purchased by Warbirds of Great Britain. Of the 27 Bearcats for which we could find civil registrations, 12 have been destroyed in crashes. Currently, around nine Bearcats are flying while another five are in various states of restoration

Right While on a May 1985 photo sortie, Howard Pardue displays the Bearcat against a cloud near the fighter's Duxford base. The aircraft carries the insignia of the Navy's famous VF-11 'Red Rippers' squadron, although its lighter-shade of gloss blue overall is far from authentic

Turkeys and Waterfowl

Above At one time, Kermit Weeks owned three Ducks, but one of the machines was traded to the United States Air Force Museum. N1214N is kept in flying condition while another example remains stored. The first of 27 JF-1s was delivered in May 1934 and all examples were in service with Navy and Marine units by early February 1935. With the J2F-6, production of the Duck switched to Columbia Aircraft and that company built all 330 J2F-6s. The -6 was essentially similar to the J2F-5 but was fitted with an R-1820-54 of 1050 hp. N1214N is maintained in very stock condition and Kermit has water landed the Duck several times

Right The Grumman J2F Duck was one of the Navy's most rugged utility amphibians, and an aircraft that firmly established the company on the aeronautical map. The company's XJF-1 made its first flight in April 1933 and the type was produced in a series of variants that featured different engines, a slight redesign and varied equipment fits. The prototype was powered by a Pratt & Whitney R-1830-62 radial of 700 hp. Currently, the only flying Ducks are examples that were built under licence by Columbia Aircraft Corporation and Kermit Weeks is seen flying his J2F-6 N1214N near his Weeks Air Museum, located at Tamiami, Florida

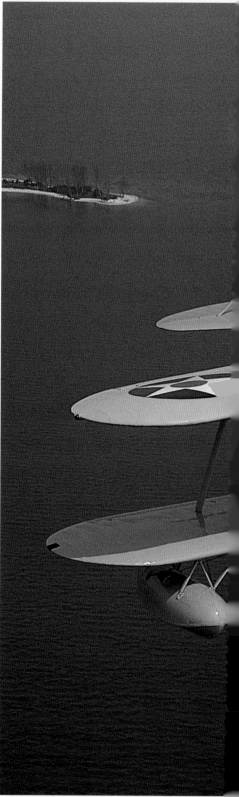

Above With the big cowling, visibility forward is rather limited during take-off as can be seen in this view. Grumman built 315 Ducks of various marks between April 1933 and March 1942, while Columbia's 330 J2F-6s were built during 1942–45. After the war, a few Ducks were sold surplus and continued their utility duties

Right Certainly one of the most effective combat aircraft of World War 2 was the Grumman TBF Avenger torpedo bomber. First flown just four months before Pearl Harbor, the TBF would receive the name Avenger early in 1942 from Grumman employees. The Avenger was created by a 1939 Bureau of Aeronautics proposal which requested an aircraft that could attack heavy surface ships with torpedoes or bombs, have a scouting capability, be able to lay a smoke screen, and be able to attack and strafe light surface vessels. However, like the Wildcat, the only Avengers flying today are those built by Eastern under licence as TBMs. Howard Pardue is seen flying TBM-3E (BuNo 53522) NX88HP (ex-N7410C), which during the 1960s had been used for ejection seat testing by Stencel Aero Engineering

Above With the gear down, Bob Pond heads TBM-3E (BuNo 53785)
NL7075C back to Chino for landing. The aircraft is finished in Royal Navy Fleet
Air Arm D-Day markings. This Avenger had been operated for many years as a
crop sprayer by Charles Reeder of Twin Falls, Idaho, before being sold for
restoration. A contract for 1200 Avengers was issued to Eastern on 23 March
1942 and the first aircraft were built from parts supplied by Grumman, but
Eastern would go on to assume complete responsibility for building the TBM.
It is interesting to note just how rapidly America adjusted to mass production,
the first 60 TBF-1s being delivered by Grumman during June 1942, the month
in which the type made its combat debut

Right One of the nicest of the restored Avengers is TBM-3E (BuNo 85886)
N9568Z which, when photographed during September 1986, was owned by
Dr John Kelly. Avengers made their debut in the Battle of Midway when six
aircraft from VT-8 attacked the Japanese fleet. However, only one Avenger
survived. It was not a good debut, but the Avenger would go on to prove
its worth

Above Coke Stuart, a retired USAF fighter pilot who passed away in January 1992, restored several aircraft to pristine condition, but the Avenger was his favourite. Grumman went on to build a total of 2290 Avengers while Eastern finished 2882 TBM-1s and 4664 TBM-3s. The Avenger is something of a contradiction since it is both sleek and portly at the same time. This is probably due to the fat fuselage which housed three crew members, a gun turret, and the torpedo. The wing of the Avenger is large but has a rather elegant sweepback to the outer panels, which helps dispel the heavy lines of the fuselage

Left Coke Stuart brings his Avenger, finished in the markings of an aircraft flown by Lt(jg) George Bush during World War 2, in close to the 'camera-ship'. TBM-3E (BuNo 85794) NL7001C had been used as a crop sprayer during the 1960s – a time when the average value of the Avenger was very low. This particular aircraft was used during Bush's inaugural parade in Washington DC and was placed on a float alongside the surviving members of Bush's torpedo squadron

Above Virtually all surplus Avengers were modified for the aerial spraying or fire fighting role. The Avenger, in fact, became the first aerial fire attack aircraft when Otto Timm and Paul Mantz installed a tank in the bomb bay and proved the effectiveness of the type in fighting Californian fires. At one time, over 60 Avenger fire bombers were in operation, but a ban on single-engined aircraft by the Forest Service put an end to the Avenger's secondary career in 1973. At this time, many aircraft went to Canada to become spruce bud worm sprayers, since this was the only market left open for the veterans, the average sale price being $5000. Today, restorers have a long and difficult search ahead of them if they want to fit original equipment such as bomb bay doors and turrets to their Avengers. TBM-3E (BuNo 53454) NL7030C, formerly tanker 13 with Reeder Flying Service, had recently been restored back to basically stock condition when photographed over Breckenridge, Texas, during May 1990

Left Gear down, TBM-3E (BuNo 53353) N526V displays the large bomb bay doors required to cover a single USN aerial torpedo. This aircraft was operated by the Georgia Forestry Commission during the 1960s and is now owned by Wiley Sanders of Troy, Alabama, and is seen over his home town during July 1990. The Royal Navy's Fleet Air Arm received 958 Tarpons (later changed to Avenger) under Lend-Lease during World War 2. The Avenger was also operated by many other foreign air arms

Above This is how most Avengers earned their keep during the 1960s. Hemet Valley Flying Service operated a large fleet of orange-painted Avengers for fire bombing and TBM-3E (BuNo 69293) N9679C tanker 96E is seen at the company's Hemet, California, base on 23 October 1967. The many modifications for the fire bombing role are evident including the removal of bomb bay doors and the elimination of the turret and all associated military gear

Right Most fire bomber companies kept a large 'junk' yard of extra parts, Avenger hulks, etc in order to keep their fleet going. This completely stock TBM-3E (BuNo 53593) N5567A was kept at Sequoia Field, California, to serve as a parts source for TBM Incorporated's fleet of Avengers. As can be seen, the aircraft still wears the full markings of the New York Naval Air Reserve. The Avenger had given up quite a few bits and pieces when photographed during March 1973, but the TBM was put back into airworthy shape and ferried to the US Naval Aviation Museum at Pensacola, Florida, on 9 September 1981 as N6822C

Above This very well-worn Avenger was rescued by Ed Maloney from a movie lot that was slated for destruction. Used in several MGM wartime films, the TBM was pulled from the lot just a few days before the area was levelled. This particular aircraft has now passed to the Yankee Air Corps at Chino, where it is in line for restoration back to flying condition. This Avenger is particularly rare since the majority of its wartime equipment is still in place.

Right The hulk of a TBM-3 fire bomber is seen in Tom Reilly's storage yard at Kissimmee, Florida. Obtained in Arizona, the aircraft will eventually be restored back to flying condition and the photograph illustrates the dedication of today's warbird restorers

After the war, Avengers soldiered on in a variety of second-line duties, operating until 1954 with the Fleet and longer with the Reserves. TBM-3E (BuNo 69329) N700RW (ex-N73642) is finished in colourful post-war utility squadron markings and the modified canopy was fitted to some Avengers that were utilized for COD (carrier onboard delivery) missions, and designated TBM-3Rs or 3Us. This aircraft flew as tanker 23 with Reeder Flying Service at Twin Falls, Idaho, during the 1960s and then lapsed into dereliction before being rescued for restoration. N700RW is owned and operated by the Lone Star Flight Museum, Galveston, Texas. Approximately 35 Avengers remain airworthy today, while around a dozen are under restoration and another 20 are on display in museums

Up on its step and just about ready to achieve flight is Grumman HU-16E (USCG serial 7226) N226CG with Ronnie Gardner and Wiley Sanders at the controls. The big Albatross is owned by Connie Edwards and is one of a small but gradually growing number of HU-16s appearing on the US civil register. Grumman Design 64 was initiated in April 1944 for a large twin-engined amphibian to undertake a variety of tasks and have an all-weather capability. The prototype was designated the XJR2F-1 and named Pelican. First flight took place on 1 October 1947. The United States Coast Guard operated 83 Albatrosses, with the first being delivered in April 1951 and the last being retired in March 1983

Above After purchasing BuNo 137297, Dennis registered the aircraft as N9722B and began the long process of bringing the Albatross back to flying condition. As can be seen, all the hard work and money paid off and the aircraft is one of the finest examples of its type still flying. The last Albatross at Guantanamo Bay was withdrawn from service and flown to Pensacola on 13 August 1976

Right Dennis Buehn brings his Albatross up on the step during take-off from Lake Tahoe on the California/Nevada border during July 1990. As a young Navy crewman, Dennis was assigned to HU-16C BuNo 137297 at NAS Guantanamo Bay in Cuba. Years later, Dennis discovered the same aircraft mouldering away in the vast Davis-Monthan AFB storage complex, and he made arrangements to purchase the Albatross. In American service, the Albatross operated with the USAF, USN, Air National Guard and Coast Guard

Grumman Design 44 was created to build a small, affordable amphibian, and the result was the Widgeon, the first example flying on 28 June 1940. Powered by two inline Ranger six-cylinder engines, the Widgeon was a success and, with the approach of World War 2, many examples were ordered by the military. A Coast Guard Widgeon sank the German U-boat U-166 off the coast of Mississippi on 1 August 1942. After the war, surplus Widgeons were eagerly snapped up and many different engine conversions were carried out to replace the not overly reliable Rangers. Widgeon N32BB was re-engined with Lycomings and is seen during May 1986. Unfortunately, shortly after this photograph was taken, the Widgeon plunged into the Pacific and exploded for no apprent reason

Above One of the rarest Grumman warbirds is the AF-2S Guardian. The aircraft was a replacement for the Avenger and Design 70 was started to create two aircraft; one that would carry all ASW gear and the other that would carry the weapons, thus creating a 'hunter-killer' team. Deliveries to the military began in mid-1950 and the Navy developed effective hunter-killer tactics with the AF-2S (killer) and AF-2W (hunter). A very large aircraft, eleven squadrons were equipped with the type until August 1955 when they were withdrawn from fleet service. Five Guardians, two AF-2Ss and three AF-2Ws, were purchased by Aero Union, and two were converted to fire bombers. One of the bombers was withdrawn from service and restored back to military condition. AF-2S (BuNo 123100) N3144G is seen during September 1974 before it was donated to the Naval Aviation Museum. One other AF-2S remains airworthy in Florida

Left Another very popular Grumman amphibian is the Goose. Design 21 was the first Grumman monoplane to fly, taking to the air on 29 May 1937. An immediate hit, the first aircraft went to the civil market but the military was not long behind and a wide variety of models were purchased starting with the JRF-1. Grumman went on to build 345 examples of the rugged Goose, and the type is still in demand today. C-FVFU, a magnificently maintained example with retractable tip floats, is seen during April 1988 on Vancouver Island where it is used in conjunction with the massive Martin JRM Mars fire bombers in the background

Another Grumman aircraft that has become popular with warbird collectors is the S-2/C-1 Tracker/Trader series. Originally designed as an ASW aircraft in 1950, the Tracker enjoyed a very long life with the US Navy, with the last aircraft not being retired until the late 1980s. Other Trackers still operate with foreign air forces while the type is also widely used for firebombing. Fresh for storage, C-1A Trader (the COD version of the design) is seen over Breckenridge, Texas, on 25 May 1991. Note the name 'Marine Crud Missle (sic)' sprayed on the nose!